Melanie Graham • Stanton Procter

English Time 4

Workbook

2nd Edition

OXFORD

UNIVERSITY PRESS

OXFORD
UNIVERSITY PRESS

Great Clarendon Street, Oxford, OX2 6DP, United Kingdom

Oxford University Press is a department of the University of Oxford.
It furthers the University's objective of excellence in research, scholarship,
and education by publishing worldwide. Oxford is a registered trade
mark of Oxford University Press in the UK and in certain other countries

© Oxford University Press 2011

The moral rights of the author have been asserted

First published in 2011

2015 2014 2013 2012
10 9 8 7 6 5 4 3

ISBN: 978 0 19 400538 8

Printed in China

This book is printed on paper from certified and well-managed sources

ACKNOWLEDGEMENTS

Cover illustration by: Paul Gibbs

Illustrations by: Mena Dolobowsky, Michelle Dorenkamp, Kate Flanagan, Ann
Iosa, Lynn Jeffery, Rita Lascaro, Susan Miller, Jon Mitchell/Beehive Illustration,
Vilma Ortiz-Dillon, Mark Ruffle, Andrew Shiff.

Original characters developed by: Amy Wummer

A. Read and match.

1. Excuse me. Can you help me? •   • Me, too. Let's have a snack.

2. How much are these? •   • 23 Plain Road.

3. I'm hungry. •   • Sure.

4. What's your address? •   • My watch!

5. Where's the trash can? •   • They're one dollar each.

6. What are you looking for? •   • It's over there. It's under the tree.

B. Read and write.

1. 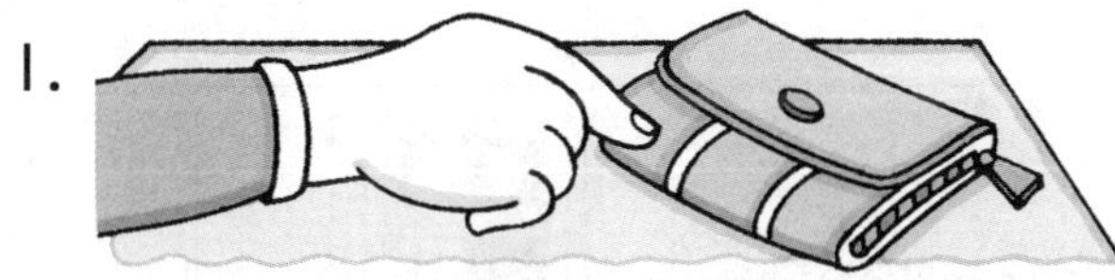

Is this a wallet?

Yes, it is. _________________

____

2. 

Is that a river?

No, it isn't. It's _____________

_________________________________ .

3. 

Are these bean sprouts?

____

____

4. 

Is that a puppy?

____

____

5. 

Is he exercising?

____

____

6. 

Was she at the bookstore?

____

____

C. Look, read, and write ✓ or ✗.

1. 

He wants eggs.
He doesn't want pasta.

2. 

How do they go to school?
They go to school by bicycle.

3. 

Whose keys are these?
They're mine.

4. 

Was she in the yard?
Yes, she was.

5. 

It was at the restaurant.
It wasn't at the museum.

6. 

When does he have a snack?
He has a snack in the afternoon.

7. 

There are some trees.
There isn't any snow.

8. 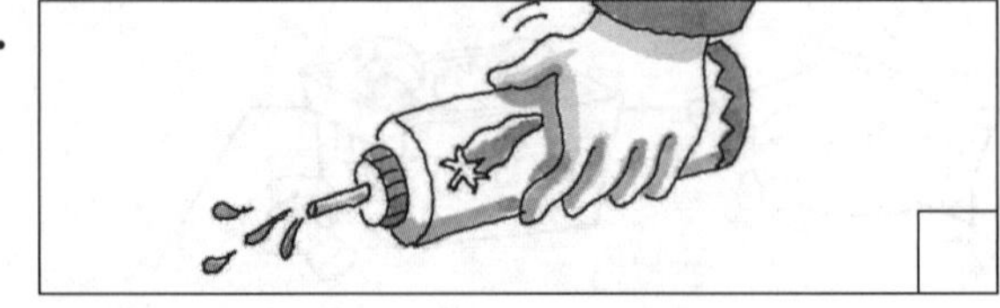

Is there any hot sauce?
No, there isn't.

D. Look and write.

1. 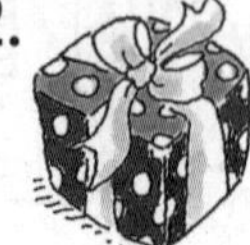 2.  3.  4.  5.  6.

1. _____ab

2. _____esent

3. _____ile

4. _____ake

5. air_____ane

6. _____ead

A. Read and circle.

1. Wake up, / Watch TV, | Annie!

2. What | time / night | is it, Penny?

3. It's | three / seven | o'clock. It's time for | school. / breakfast.

4. Good. I'm | hungry. / happy.

5. Looks / Smells | good. What's for | breakfast? / homework?

6. We're having | bread / bird | and | eggs. / ears.

7. Yum! | Their / My | favorite!

B. Read and match.

1. What's for breakfast?
   We're having cheese and bread.

2. What's for breakfast?
   We're having rice, fish, and fruit.

3. What's for breakfast?
   We're having cereal and juice.

A. Read and circle.

1. 

climb / cook — a / an — computer / **mountain**
(circled: climb, a, mountain)

2. 

listen / laugh — at / to — stories / sunrise

3. 

climb / clean — the / to — pans / tent

4. 

wash / watch — the / your — sunrise / pots

5. 

play / bake — cards / jokes

6. 

cook / call — bedroom / breakfast

B. Look and write.

1. 

I'm watching ________________________________
________________________________ .

2. 

He isn't washing ________________________________
________________________________ .

3. 

We're ________________________________
________________________________ .

4. 

She's ________________________________
________________________________ .

A. **Write the questions and answers.**

1. you  ? 

Did you play cards?
No, I didn't. I ________
________.

2. he  ? 

3. she  ? 

4. they  ? 

B. **Read and write.**

1. Did they cook breakfast?

____

2. Did she laugh at jokes?

____

3. _________________

Yes, he did.

4. _________________

Yes, they did.

A. Circle and write.

1. 

ch
th
sh

____irt

2. 

pr
br
dr

____esent

3. 

sl
pr
pl

air____ane

4. 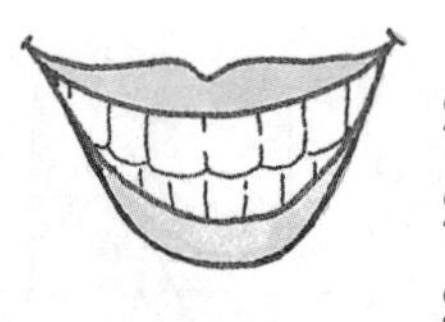

sm
sn
sp

____ile

5. 

gr
tr
sh

____ee

6. 

fl
cr
sl

____ower

7.

cr
dr
ch

____air

8. **3**

th
br
tr

____ree

B. Read and write. Use some letters twice.

| tr | gr | pl | tch | th | sm | sp | fl | sh | cr | ch |

We like this park. There are ____owers and ____ees.
There is ____een ____ass. We ____y kites and ____ay
on the slide. We wa____ the fi____ in the ____eek
and catch ____iders. Our mo____ers ____ile and eat
pea____es and ____ums.

A. Unscramble and write. Then number the sentences in the correct order.

have / I / money. / Uh-oh! / don't / enough

____

so / really / It's / I'm / thirsty. / hot.

_1_ ____

a / Thanks / lot.

____

get / Let's / too. / Me, / juice. / some

____

do / kind / What / juice / of / want? / you

____

treat. / That's / It's / okay. / my

____

Here / are. / you

____

juice, / Orange / please.

____

B. Your turn. What do you want? Read and write.

I'm _______________________________ .

I want _____________________________ .

A. Unscramble and write. Then number the words.

krind aosd opp

_______ _______________________

tae tocnot yndac

_______ _______________________

og on a dire

_______ _______________________

yub ckttsie

_______ _______________________

aket sciprute

_______ _______________________

niw a eripz

_______ _______________________

veah chunl

_______ _______________________

ees a hows

_______ _______________________

B. Look and write.

1. <u>I have lunch at twelve o'clock.</u>

2. I _______________________.

3. _______________________

4. _______________________

5. _______________________

6. _______________________

A. **Read and write.**

1. drink ⟶ ___drank___

2. eat ⟶ _____________

3. win ⟶ _____________

4. go ⟶ _____________

5. see ⟶ _____________

6. have ⟶ _____________

7. buy ⟶ _____________

8. take ⟶ _____________

B. **Look and write. Then number the pictures.**

1. I _____________ on a ride. I didn't _____________ pictures.

2. I _____________ tickets. I didn't _____________ a prize.

3. I _____________ pictures. I didn't _____________ cotton candy.

C. **Look and write.**

1. 

She went on a ride.

She didn't _____________.

2. 

He _____________.

_____________.

3. 

They _____________.

_____________.

A. Which word has a different -ed sound? Read and circle.

1.
walked
played
asked

2.
baked
called
cleaned

3.
climbed
talked
chopped

4.
used
washed
danced

B. Read and write. Then write the words in the correct category.

1. brush ⟶ __brushed__

2. water ⟶ __________

3. kiss ⟶ __________

4. watch ⟶ __________

5. pull ⟶ __________

6. play ⟶ __________

7. laugh ⟶ __________

8. listen ⟶ __________

walked

____
____
____
____

used

____
____
____
____

C. Read the word. Then circle the words with the same -ed sound.

1. played

On Monday, Lisa watered the plants and brushed her hair.
Then she called a friend.

2. asked

On Saturday, Ted and Annie listened to music. They baked
cookies, too. Then they washed the pots and pans.

A. Unscramble and write.

1.

 eLt em hlpe oyu, moM.

____

 haTkns. eB farcelu. t'Is eahvy.

____

2.

 oN emporbl. m'I rostgn.

____

 eYs, ouy rae.

____

3.

 pelH!

____

 atWhc tou!

____

4.

 rAe ouy koya?

____

 I htkin os, ubt olok ta ym

broasakted. _______________________________

____

B. Read and match.

1. Be back by six!

2. Be careful!

3. Sh! Be quiet!

A. Use the code to write the words. Then match.

m	n	o	p	q	r	s	t	u	v	w	x	y	z	a	b	c	d	e	f	g	h	i	j	k	l
↓	↓	↓	↓	↓	↓	↓	↓	↓	↓	↓	↓	↓	↓	↓	↓	↓	↓	↓	↓	↓	↓	↓	↓	↓	↓
a	b	c	d	e	f	g	h	i	j	k	l	m	n	o	p	q	r	s	t	u	v	w	x	y	z

1. __sweep__ the __floor__
   eiqqb   rxaad

2. _______ the _______
   pa   xmgzpdk

3. _______ the _______
   tmzs gb   oxaftqe

4. _______ the _______
   ymwq   nqp

5. _______ the _______
   eqf   fmnxq

6. _______ the _______
   fmwq agf   smdnmsq

7. _______ the _______
   bgf mimk   sdaoqduqe

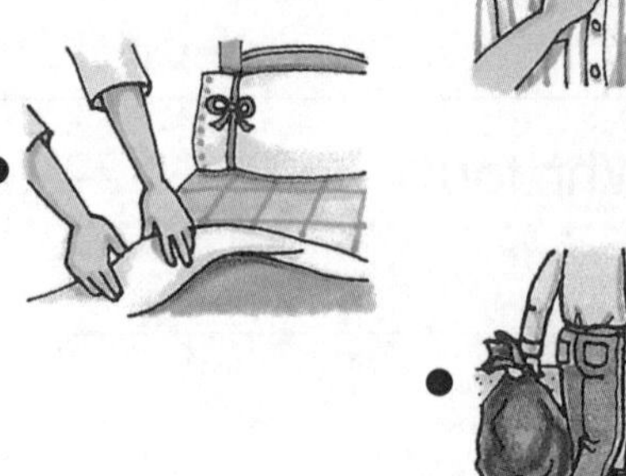

B. Read and write.

1. 

What's she doing?

____

____

2. 

What's he doing?

____

____

3. 

What are they doing?

____

____

A. Read and match.

1. What did you do?
   I swept the floor.

2. What did you do?
   I hung up the clothes.

3. What did you do?
   We did the laundry.

B. Look, read, and write.

1. What did she do?

____

____

2. What did they do?

____

____

3. What _______________________ ?

____

____

4. _______________________________

____

____

5. _______________________________

____

____

6. _______________________________

____

____

A. Read the word. Then circle the words with the same -ed sound.

1. shouted   kissed   invited   weeded   played

2. cooked   watched   waited   planned   counted

3. greeted   chopped   dusted   planted   washed

B. Read and answer the questions.

Moe was busy on Saturday. In the morning, he played the piano and painted a picture. He called his friends, Sue and Jack, and invited them for lunch. Jack roasted some chicken. They ate under a tree. "Look at this," said Moe. "I planted a seed and now it's a tree!" In the afternoon, Moe, Sue, and Jack weeded the garden. Then they cleaned up.

1. Who did Moe invite for lunch?

2. When did Moe paint a picture?

3. Did Moe plant a weed?

4. What did Moe, Sue, and Jack do in the afternoon?

5. What did Jack roast?

A. Match and write.

1. Are you okay? •
2. I don't have enough money. •
3. I'm really thirsty. •
4. Let me help you. •
5. What's for breakfast? •

• I __________ so.

• We're __________ bread and eggs.

• __________. Be __________.

• Me, too. __________ get some __________.

• That's __________. It's my __________.

B. What did you do? Look and write.

| morning | afternoon | evening | night |

1. I fed the pets in the morning.

2. I __________.

3. __________

4. __________

5. __________

6. __________

7. __________

8. __________

A. Read and write.

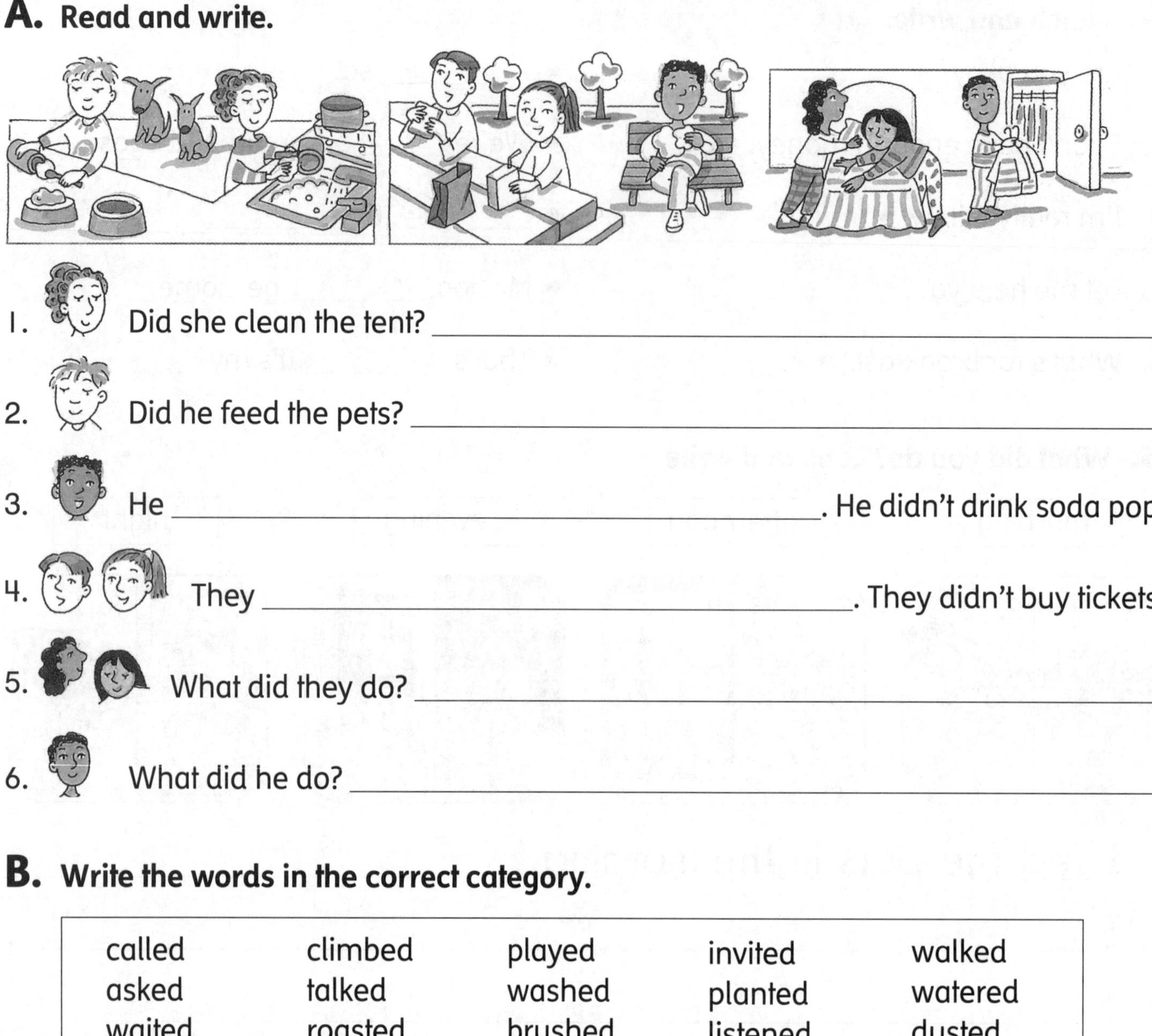

1. Did she clean the tent? _______________________________

2. Did he feed the pets? _______________________________

3. He _______________________________. He didn't drink soda pop.

4. They _______________________________. They didn't buy tickets.

5. What did they do? _______________________________

6. What did he do? _______________________________

B. Write the words in the correct category.

called	climbed	played	invited	walked
asked	talked	washed	planted	watered
waited	roasted	brushed	listened	dusted

clean**ed**	cook**ed**	weed**ed**

A. Read and circle.

1. 

broke his hand
burned his hand

2. 

cut her finger
strained her finger

3. 

broke his arm
cut his arm

4. 

burned her knee
strained her knee

5. 

bandage
cast

6. 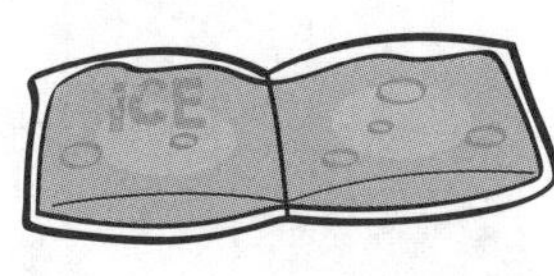

antibiotic ointment
ice pack

7. 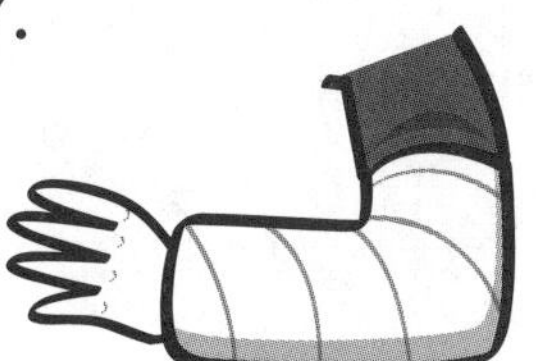

ice pack
cast

8. 

bandage
antibiotic ointment

B. Read and write.

1. 

He _______________ his leg.

The doctor put a _______________ on it.

2. 

She _______________________________.

She _______________________________.

3. 

He _______________________________.

He _______________________________.

4. 

She _______________________________.

She _______________________________.

A. **Fill in the blanks. Use some words twice.**

looking	Thank	really	you
You're	Walk	left	fun
museum	turn	right	far

1.  Excuse me. I'm __________ for the __________. Is it __________?

2.  Not __________.

3.  __________ two blocks. Turn __________. It's on the right.

4. Did you say turn right or __________ __________?

5.  Turn __________. It's on the __________.

6.  __________ __________ very much.

7.  __________ welcome. Have __________!

B. **Read and match.**

1. Walk two blocks. Turn left. It's on the left.

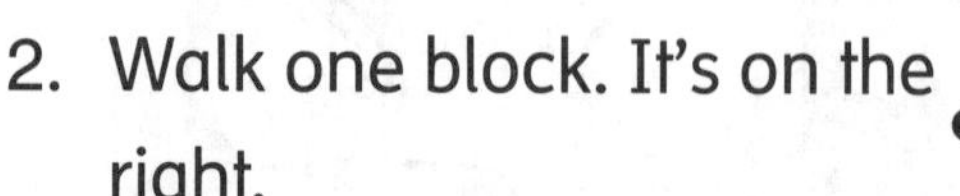

2. Walk one block. It's on the right.

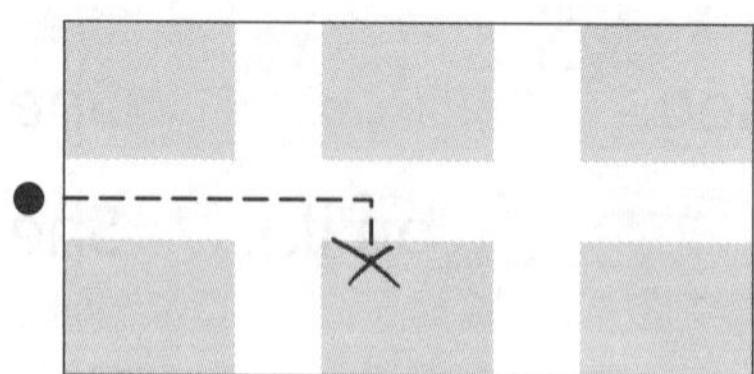

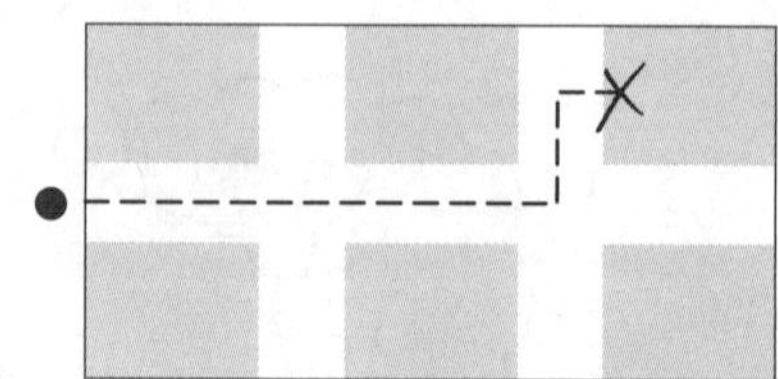

3. Walk two blocks. Turn left. It's on the right.

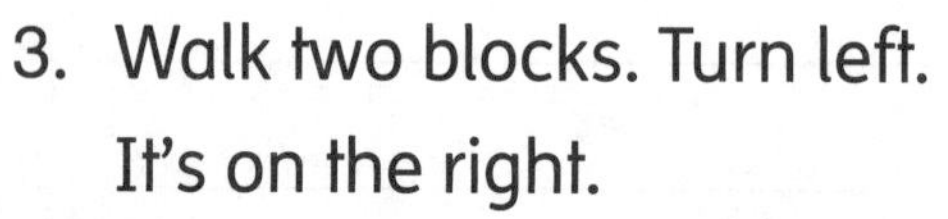

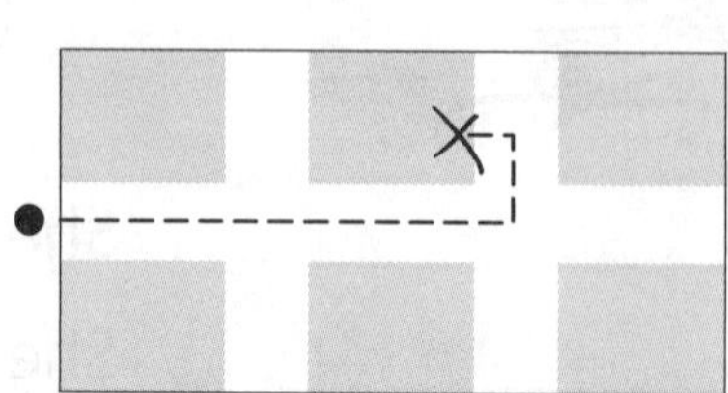

A. Unscramble and write.

teg a tuhcair	lami a telter	isitv a ndrief
yub a tdoun	keat a xiat	tren a VDD

1. 

2. 

3. 

4. 

5. 

6. 

B. What are they doing? Look and write.

1. They're riding the bus.

2. He's getting ____________.

3. She's ____________.

4. She's ____________.

5. They're ____________.

6. He's ____________.

A. Read. Then write ✓ and ✗.

1. 

She's going to take a taxi.
She isn't going to ride the bus.

2. 

They're going to see a movie.
They aren't going to rent a DVD.

3. 

I'm going to mail a letter.
I'm not going to visit a friend.

4. 

We're going to buy a donut.
We aren't going to get a haircut.

B. Look and write.

1.  

She's ______________ visit a friend.
______________ take a taxi.

______________ take a taxi.
______________ visit a friend.

2.  

____

____

____

____

A. Complete the puzzle.

Across →

2. 
5. 
7.

Down ↓

1. 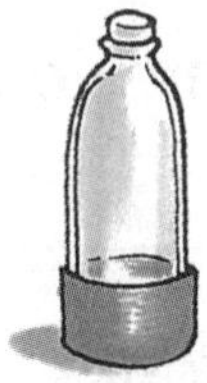
3. 
4. 
6.

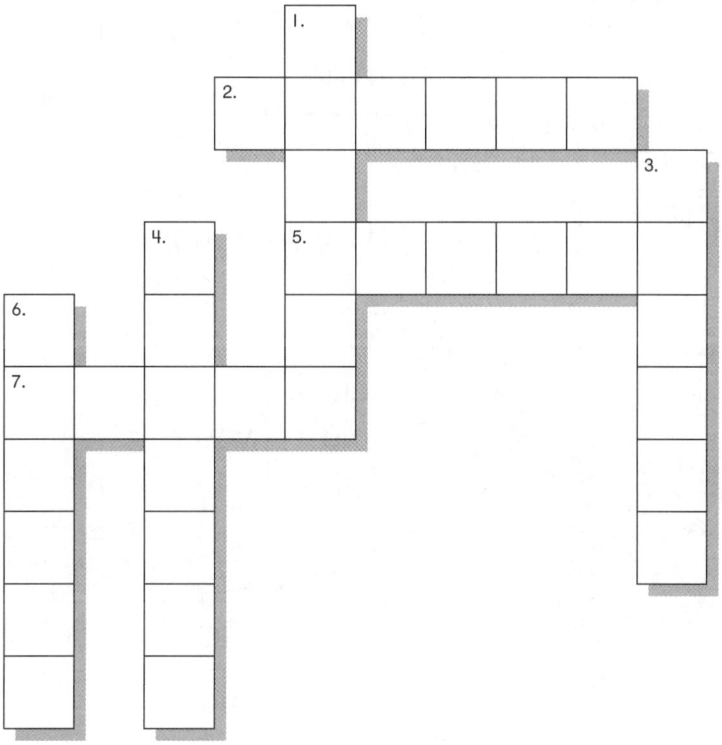

B. Read and circle the -le words.

Lana's uncle gave her a saddle. She rode her horse and
saw some cattle. She jumped in the lake and made a ripple.
She swam to the middle and saw a turtle.

"Little girl, give me an apple," said the turtle.

"I don't have an apple," said Lana, "but I have a saddle."

5

A. Read and circle.

What are you | eat? / ate? / eating?

Rice. | Try / Trying / Tried | some. It's good.

No, | thanks. / thank. / thanked.

Come / Came / Coming | on. Just a little.

Oh, all right. But not too much.

Here you | went. / going. / go.

Hey! | Its / It's / Is | delicious!

I | telling / told / tell | you so!

B. Read and match.

1. What is she drinking?
   Apple juice.

2. What are you eating?
   Popcorn.

3. What are you drinking?
   Soda pop.

4. What are they eating?
   Bread and eggs.

A. Read and circle.

1. 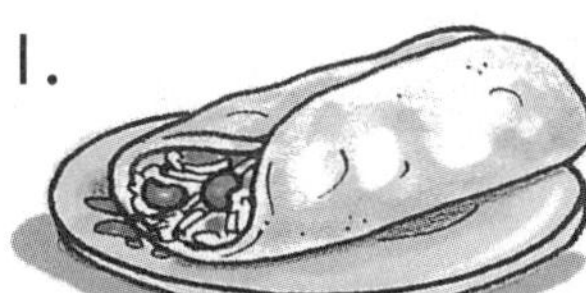
a burrito
hot dogs

2. 
a taco
tacos

3. 
curry
iced tea

4. 
french fries
spaghetti

5. 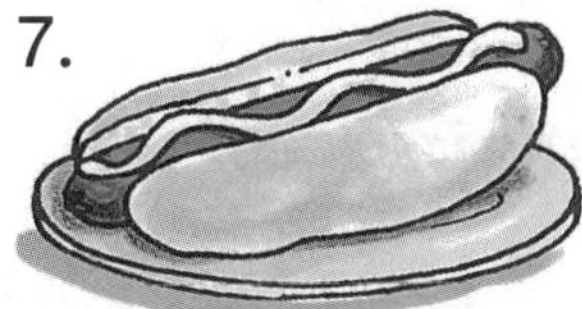
lemonade
iced tea

6. 
spaghetti
burritos

7. 
a french fry
a hot dog

8. 
lemonade
curry

B. Look and write.

1. 

I want _______________ .

I don't want _______________ .

2. 

She _______________ .

3. 

____

____

4. 

____

____

C. Your turn. Read and write.

____

____

A. Read and match.

What are you going to have?

What are they going to have?

What's he going to have?

What's she going to have?

We're going to have some iced tea.

He's going to have a burrito.

They're going to have some curry.

She's going to have a taco.

B. Look and write.

1. What's _____________ ?
He's _____________ .

2. _____________

3. _____________

4. _____________

A. Fill in the blanks.

paper	eraser	blister	ruler
marker	Peter	finger	computer

My name is _____________. I have a _____________ on my _____________. I have a _____________ on my desk. I have some _____________ in my desk. I don't have an _____________, but I have a _____________ and a _____________.

B. Fill in the blanks.

father
sister
lobster
peppers
butter
mother
cucumber
water
brother
dinner

It's time for _____________ at my house. My _____________ is going to have a burger. My _____________ is going to have a _____________. My _____________ is going to have _____________ with _____________. My _____________ is going to have roasted _____________. Digger is going to have some _____________.

6

A. Find the words. Then fill in the blanks and match.

acrossexcusetimeyourfavoritemaththanksfunsubjectmusiclibraryclass

1. What's _____________
   favorite _____________?   •

2. _____________ me. Where's
   the _____________?   •

3. _____________.   •

4. Oh! It's _____________ for
   art _____________.   •

   • Go straight. It's _____________
   from the _____________ room.

   • I like _____________. It's
   _____________.

   • Great! That's my
   _____________.

   • Sure.

B. Look at the chart. Write the questions and answers.

	Ted	Annie	Bob and Jan
Subject	English	math	English
Animal	lizard	dog	fish
Color	blue	red	green

1. What's Annie's favorite animal? She likes dogs.

2. _____________ color? _____________

3. _____________ subject? _____________

4. _____________ animal? _____________

A. Look and match. Then write the phrases in the correct category.

1.  2.  3.  4.  5.  6.

go · plant · pick · build · go · play

a snowman · flowers · in the leaves · skiing · to the beach · apples

winter	
spring	
summer	
fall	

B. Look and write.

1. 

It's _______. I'm going to go to the beach.

2. 

It's _______. I'm going to _______.

3. 

4. 

A. Read and circle True or False.

1.		He'll go skiing in the winter. He won't pick apples.	True	False
2.		He'll go to the beach in the summer. He won't plant flowers.	True	False
3.		She'll build a snowman in the fall. She won't pick apples.	True	False
4.		She'll plant flowers in the spring. She won't play in the leaves.	True	False

B. Look and write.

1. 

He'll _______________________.

He won't _______________________.

2. 

____

____

3.

____

____

C. Your turn. What will you do?

I'll _______________________. I _______________________.

A. Circle and write.

1. 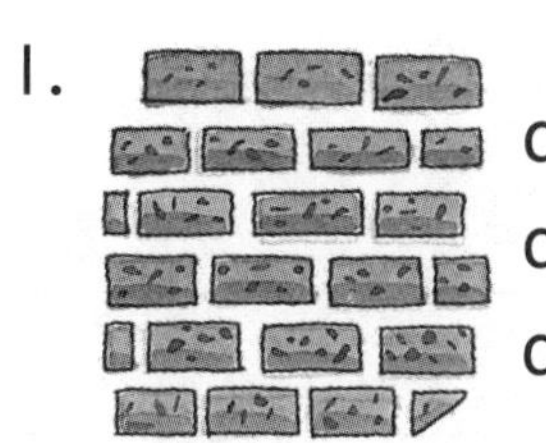
al
au
aw

w____l

2. 
al
au
aw

dr______

3. 
al
au
aw

s______cer

4. 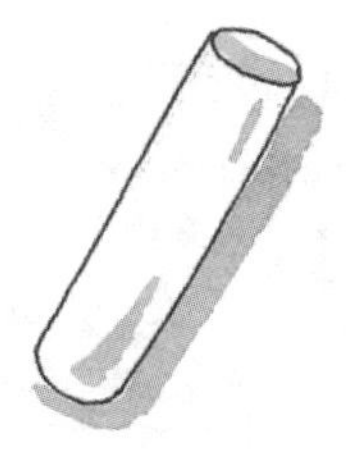
al
au
aw

ch______k

5. 
al
au
aw

t____k

6. 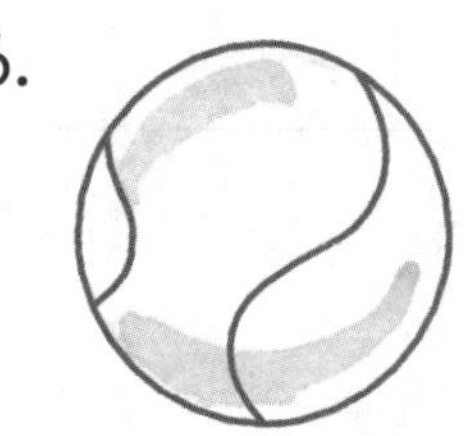
al
au
aw

b______l

7. 
al
au
aw

cr______l

8. 
al
au
aw

w______k

B. Read and write.

1. Paul can't walk. Can he crawl?

____

2. Does Paul draw on the wall with crayons?

____

3. Who sees Paul draw?

____

4. Does Paul like to draw on the wall?

____

A. Read and write.

1. Excuse me. Where's the library?
Go straight. It's ______________________
_________________________________ .

2. _________________________________
____
I like math. It's fun.

3. What are you eating?
Rice. Try _______________________ .
____

4. _________________________________
____
I told you so.

B. Match and write.

1. see •   • a donut
2. visit •   • a friend
3. mail •   • a haircut
4. build •   • a movie   **see a movie**
5. take •   • a taxi
6. get •   • a snowman
7. rent •   • a letter
8. buy •   • a DVD

A. Look and write.

1. 

He's going to _______________________.
He isn't _______________________.

2. 

____
____

B. Look and write.

1.  

What are you going to have?
____

2.  

____
____

C. Look and write.

1. 

She'll plant flowers _______________________.
She won't _______________________.

2. 

____
____

D. Look and write.

1.    2.    3. 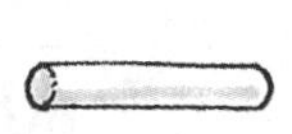   4.    5.    6. 

lobst______   tig______   ch______k   pudd______   s______cer   beet______

A. Read and circle.

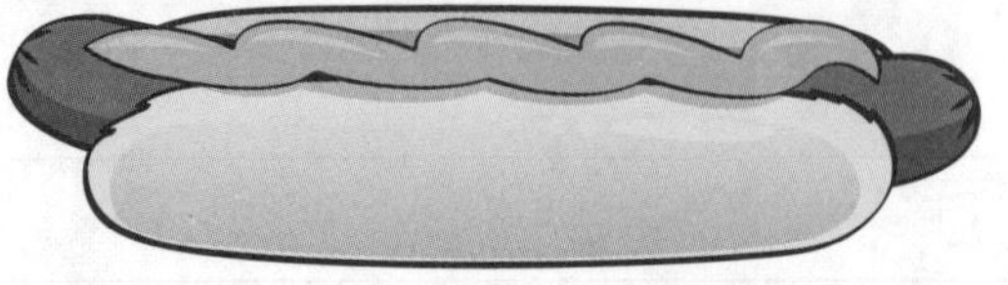

There were eight people at Jim's birthday party. Each person ate two hot dogs. How many hot dogs did they eat?

1. This is | an equation. / a word problem.

2. This is a | division / multiplication | problem.

3. Eight | multiplied / divided | by two equals | sixteen. / four.

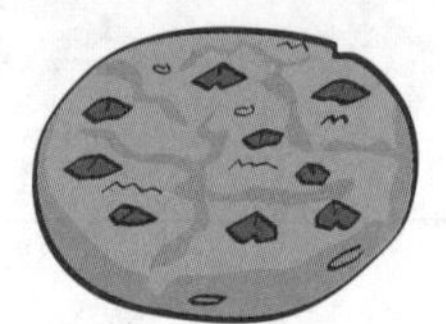

Matt baked twenty cookies. He took the cookies to school for two friends. How many cookies did each friend get?

4. This is a | division / multiplication | problem.

5. Twenty | divided / multiplied | by two equals | ten. / eight.

6. The equation is: | 20 x 2 = 40 / 20 ÷ 2 = 10

B. Read and write.

1.

Look at this word problem:

Three people give Amy five dollars for her birthday. How much money does Amy have?

This is a _______________ problem. Three _______________ by five equals _______________.

The equation is: _______________

2.

Look at this word problem:

Leo has twelve dollars. One ride is three dollars. How many rides can he go on?

This is a _______________ problem. Twelve _______________ by three equals _______________.

The equation is: _______________

7

A. Number the sentences in the correct order.

_____ Well, it's time to go.
Please make up your mind.

_____ Oh, I don't know. They're all cute.

_____ Great! Let's get it.

_____ Are you sure?

_____ Um, okay. I'll take this one.

_____ I'm positive!

_____ Dad, the cashier is over here.

_____ Which one do you want?

B. Look and match.

1. 
2. 
3. 
4. 

Which one do you want?

I'll take that one.

I don't know.

I'll take this one.

A. Look. Then write the letter.

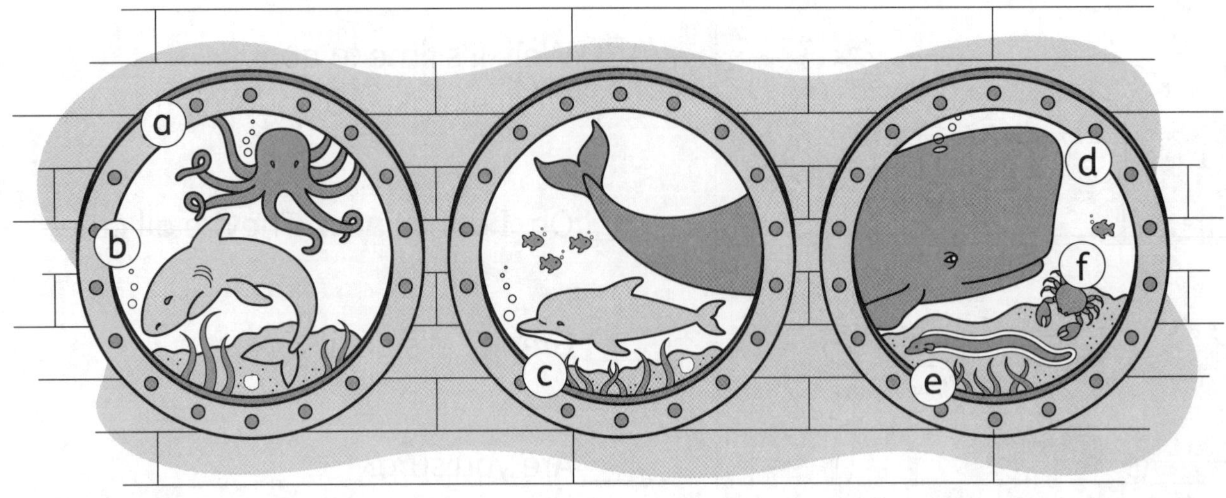

1. whale _____ 2. eel _____ 3. dolphin _____

4. octopus _____ 5. shark _____ 6. crab _____

B. Look and write.

1.

a big whale

a _______________

2.

C. Your turn. Read and write.

A. Read and write True or False.

1. The octopus is slower than the dolphin.   _____True_____

2. The dolphin is bigger than the shark.   __________

3. The eel is smaller than the whale.   __________

4. The whale is faster than the crab.   __________

5. The shark is slower than the octopus.   __________

6. The whale is bigger than the dolphin.   __________

B. Look and write.

1. 

2. 

3. 
4. 

1. fast   The _______________ faster than _______________ .

2. slow _______________

3. big _______________

4. small _______________

A. Circle and write **ar** or **or**. Then number the pictures.

1.
ar   or

f_____m

2.
ar   or

c_____n

3.
ar   or

st_____m

4.
ar   or

b_____n

5.
ar   or

f_____k

6.
ar   or

liz_____d

 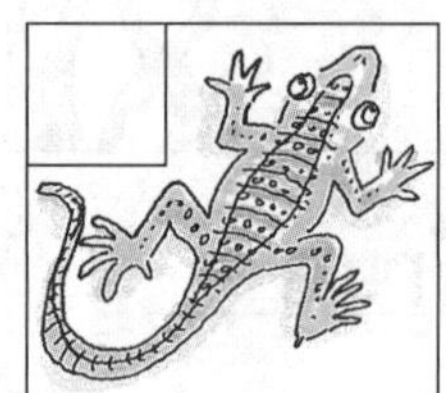 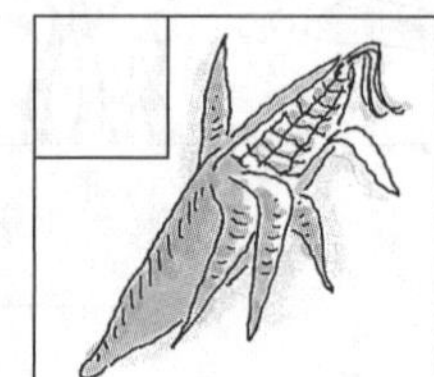   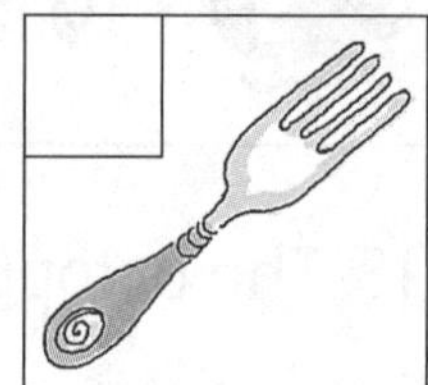

B. Fill in the blanks.

dark	farm	horse	stories	barn	corn
cards	lizard	garden	yard	storm	popcorn

Today we visited Grandpa's _______________. Grandpa grows peas and ___________ in the _______________. His _______________ lives in a big, red _______________. A small, green _______________ lives there, too. We chased it across the _______________.

There was a _______________ in the evening. It rained and the sky was _______________. We played _______________ and listened to _______________ in the house. Grandpa made _______________.

8

A. Fill in the blanks.

car	cute	Quick	What	windows	is	going
what	worry	won't	monkey	scary	Look	not

1. Dad! Guess ______________!

2. ______________?

3. There's a ______________ on the ______________!

4. ______________! Shut the ______________!

5. ______________! There it ______________.

6. Oh, it's ______________.

7. It's ______________ cute. It's ______________.

8. Don't ______________. It ______________ hurt you.

9. Aw! It's ______________ away.

B. Look and write.

1. mouse / jump / bed

Guess ______________! ______________

There's ______________________________.

Quick! Jump ______________________________.

2. lizard / shut / door

______________ ______________

____

____

A. Unscramble, write, and circle.

1. aceehht 

____

2. aeffgir 

____

3. aceehimnpz 

____

4. elrttu 

____

5. aeehlnpt 

____

6. aekns 

____

B. Look and write.

1. 

2. 

3. 

4. 

She's __________ .   __________   __________   __________

C. Look and write.

1. 

The chimpanzee is short.

2. 

____

3. 

____

4. 

____

A. Circle and write.

1. 

Which one is the / tallest / shortest / (fattest)?

The ___snake___ is the ___fattest___ .

2. 

Which one is the / thinnest / tallest / shortest ?

The _____________ is the _____________ .

3. 

Which one is the / thinnest / shortest / fattest ?

The _____________ is the _____________ .

4. 

Which one is the / slowest / fattest / tallest ?

The _____________ is the _____________ .

B. Write the questions and answers.

1. tall

Which one _______________ ?

The _______________ .

2. short

____

____

3. fat

____

____

4. thin

____

____

A. Does it have ou or ow? Look and write.

1. 
t___n

2. 
c___

3. 
m___se

4. 
cl___d

5. 
sh___t

6. 
g___n

7. 
h___se

8. 
m___th

B. Fill in the blanks. Use some words twice.

1. The mouse is climbing the ___________________.

2. The man is ___________________. His ___________________ is open.

3. There are five ___________________.

4. The ___________________ are eating the grass.

5. There are two ___________________ in the sky.

6. There is a little ___________________ on the ___________________.

9 Conversation Time

Fill in the blanks.

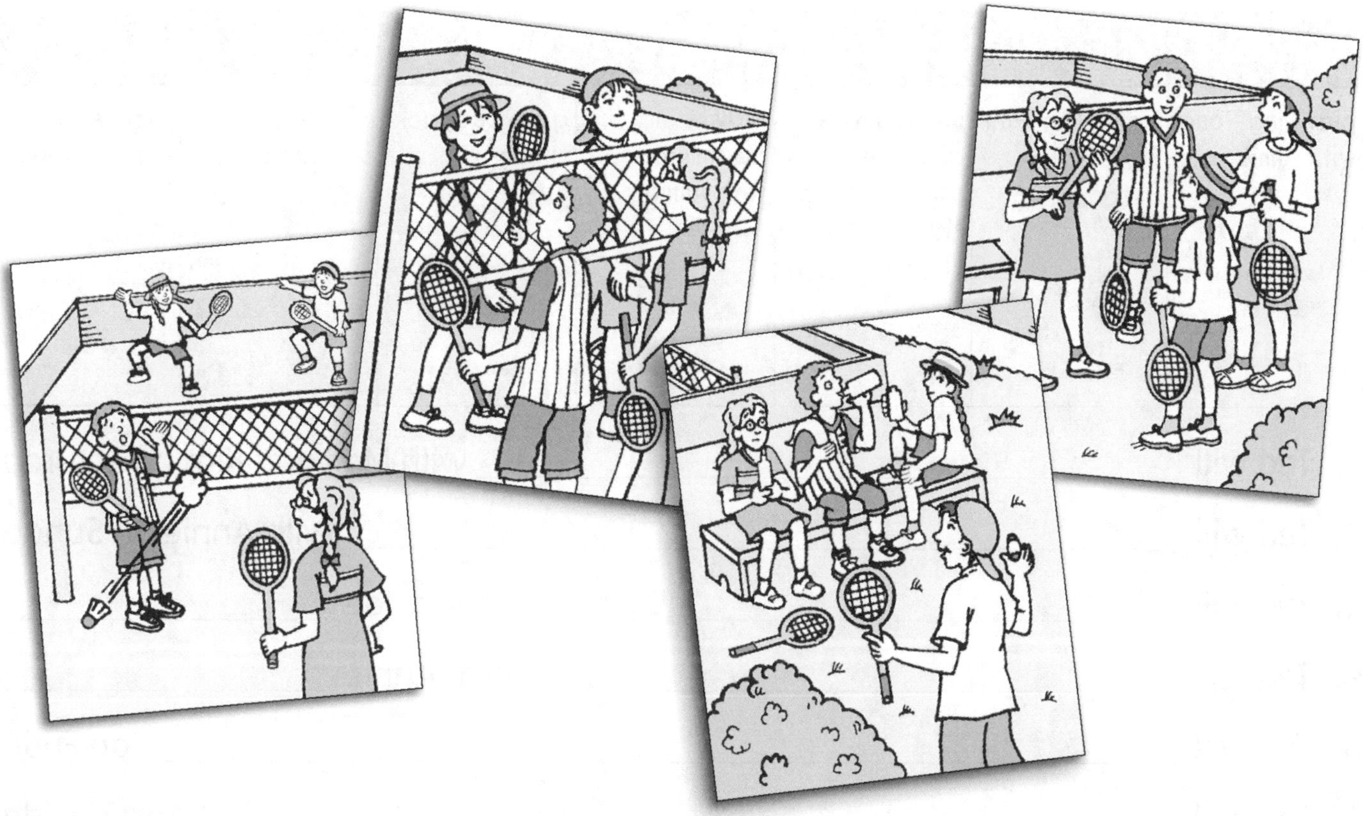

We won!	Yeah, it was.	We'll see.	And this time, we'll win.
I missed it!	It was close.	Congratulations.	Do you want to play again?

1. 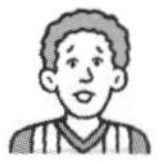 Oh, no! ______________________

2. ______________________ We won!

3. 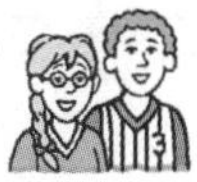 ______________________

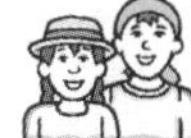

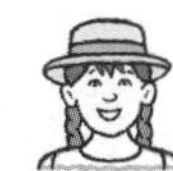

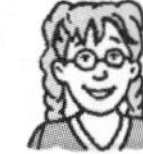

4. Nice game. ______________________

5. ______________________

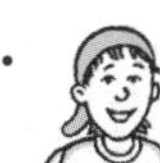

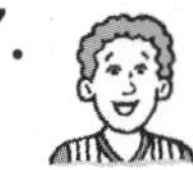

6. ______________________

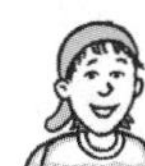

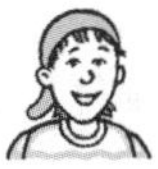

7. Sure. ______________________

8. ______________________

A. Look and read. Then write.

Sunday	Monday	Tuesday	Wednesday	Thursday	Friday	Saturday
play Ping-Pong with Annie	go sailing with Ivy	in-line skate and listen to music with Matt	play badminton with Annie	go horseback riding with Joe	go fishing with Dad	snorkel with Matt and Kim

1. Ted will ________________________ with Matt and Kim on Saturday.

2. Ted will ________________________ with Annie on Sunday.

3. Ted will ________________________ with Joe ________________.

4. Ted will ________________________ with Annie ________________.

5. Ted will ________________________ on Friday.

6. Ted will ________________________ on Tuesday.

B. Look and write.

1. 

He's going sailing.

2. 

3. 

4. 

5. 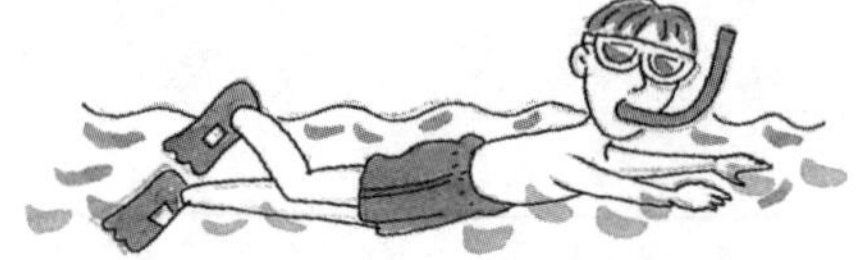

6. 

A. Read and write the words. Then write ✓.

1. What do you like to do?

   __I like__ to go horseback riding.

2. What does he like to do?

   ______________ to go sailing.

3. What do you like to do?

   ______________ to listen to music.

B. Look and write.

1.  What does she like to do?

   ____

   ____

2. What does he like to do?

   ____

   ____

3.  _______________________________

   ____

   ____

4. _______________________________

   ____

A. Which word has a different oo sound? Read and circle.

1.
spoon
moon
wood

2.
book
took
moon

3.
good
rooster
cookie

4.
foot
school
wood

5.
broom
moon
took

B. Read and match.

1. The baboon cooked some food. ●

2. The poodle and the rooster looked at the moon. ●

3. The moose stood on one foot. ●

4. She sat on the wood and read a book. ●

C. Look at B and write the oo words in the correct category.

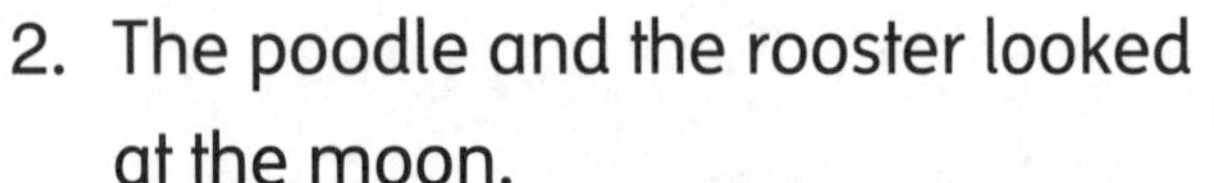

cookie

broom

_________ _________

_________ _________

_________ _________

A. Look and write.

1. 

Oh! __________________________

2. 

Um, okay. I'll take that one.

3. 

Dad, __________________________.

4. 

Aw! __________________________

B. Read and write.

1. 

Is it a giraffe?
No, it isn't.

It's a __________________________.

2. 

Is it an eel?
____

3. 

Is it a chimpanzee?
____
____

4. 

Is it a shark?
____

5. 

Is it a crab?
____
____

6. 

Is it a dolphin?
____
____

A. Read and write.

1. whale / big / elephant   <u>The whale is bigger than the elephant.</u>
2. cheetah / fast / turtle ____
3. eel / small / dolphin ____
4. crab / slow / giraffe ____

B. Look and write.

1. Which one is the ___________________? The giraffe ___________________.
2. ___________________ fattest? ___________________
3. Which one is the ___________________? The snake is the ___________________.
4. ___________________ shortest? ___________________

C. Write the words in the correct category.

oo	<u>broom</u>		ar	________		ou	________
oo	________		or	________		ow	________

A. Write the letter.

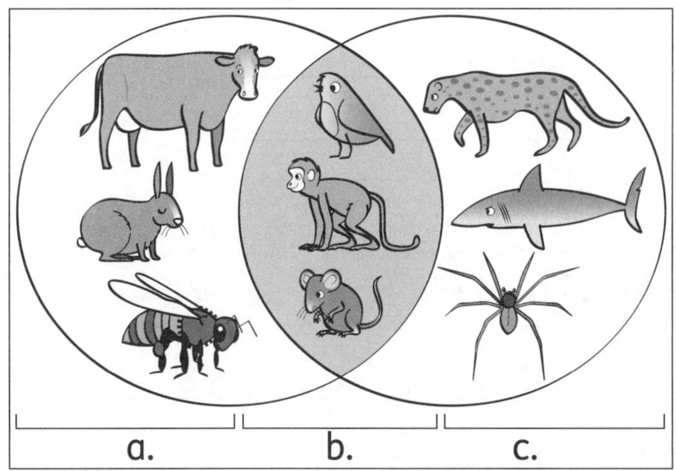

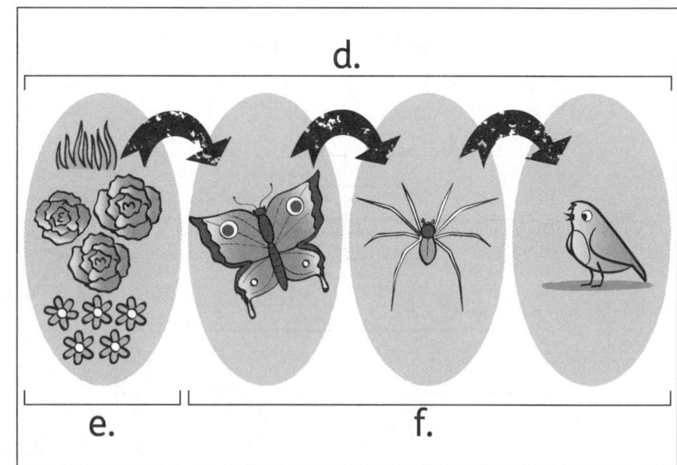

1. a food chain _______
2. producers _______
3. herbivores _______
4. consumers _______
5. omnivores _______
6. carnivores _______

B. Read and write.

1. These animals eat plants.
   They're ________________.

2. These animals eat animals.
   They're ________________.

3. These animals eat plants and animals.
   They're ________________.

4. The caterpillar eats the plant. The bird eats the caterpillar. The snake eats the bird. This is a ________________.

5. Plants are food for others.
   They're ________________.

6. Bugs, birds, and snakes eat food.
   They're ________________.

10

A. Fill in the blanks.

Wow! What a cool kite.

Thanks. ________________________
1

____
2

No, it's true. I made it.

____
3

No, it was easy. ________________________
4

Great. ________________________
5

________________________ Let's get some.
6

You're kidding!	What do we need?
Paper and string.	Was it hard?
I made it myself.	I'll show you.

B. Read and match.

1. Was it easy?
   No, it was hard.

2. What a cool kite!
   Yeah. Sara made it.

3. What do we need?
   Tape, paper, and crayons.

A. Look. Then number the words.

______ cycle   ______ read a comic book   ______ collect stickers   ______ sing

______ paint   ______ take a nap   ______ make a movie   ______ build a model

B. What will they do in the summer? Look and write.

1. 

2.

3. 

4.

5. 

6.

7. 

8.

1. He'll build a model.   2. She'll _______________.

3. _______________   4. _______________

5. _______________   6. _______________

7. _______________   8. _______________

A. Read and write. Then number the pictures.

1. _____I_____ like cycling, but _____I_____ don't like collecting stickers.

2. _______ likes making movies, but _______ doesn't like building models.

3. _______ like painting, but _______ don't like taking naps.

4. _______ likes singing, but _______ doesn't like reading comic books.

B. Look and write.

1.  She likes ________________________________, but
   she doesn't ________________________________.

2.  ________________________________
   ____

3.  ________________________________
   ____

4. ________________________________
   ____

A. Does it have er, ir, or ur? Circle and write.

1. 

er   ur   ir

b____d

2. 

ur   er   ir

c____ry

3. 

ir   ur   er

dess____t

4. 

ur   ir   er

g____l

5. 

ir   er   ur

d____ty

6. 

er   ir   ur

n____se

7. 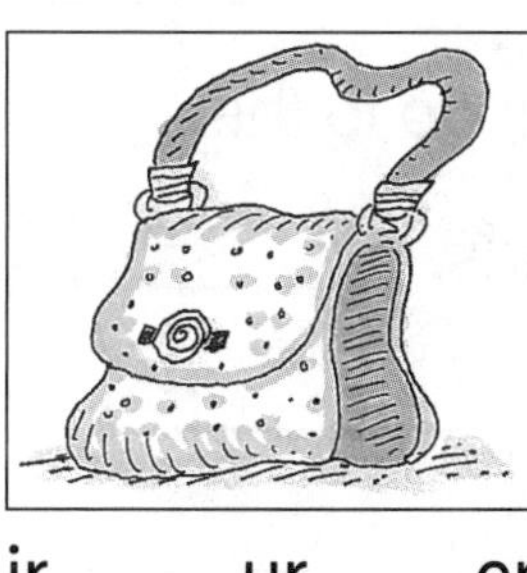

ir   ur   er

p____se

8. 

ur   er   ir

sh____t

B. Fill in the blanks.

| thirteen |
| shirt |
| dirty |
| thirsty |
| hurts |
| dessert |
| curry |
| bird |
| girl |
| purse |

1. It can fly. It's small. It's a ____________.

2. ____________ is my favorite food. I eat it with rice.

3. Chocolate cake is my favorite ____________.

4. Ted is a boy. Annie is a ____________.

5. My keys and my wallet are in my ____________.

6. The kitchen is ____________. Let's clean up.

7. I want iced tea. I'm ____________.

8. Ouch! My foot ____________!

9. Ten and three is ____________.

10. Gert bought jeans and a ____________.

11

A. Fill in the blanks. Use some words twice.

Can	No	we	hurry	thirsty	buy	show
Yeah	a	planets	the	snack	We	great
Wow	I'm	catch	stars	bus	gift	time

1. _________________! Did you see all the _________________ and _________________?

2. _________________! That was a _________________.

3. Ms. Apple, can we go to the _________________ bar?

4. _________________ we go to the _________________ shop?

5. _________________, kids. _________________ don't have _________________.

6. Aw. But I want to ____ for my dad.

7. And ____.

8. Please, Ms. Apple. We'll ____.

9. Sorry, kids. _________________ have to _________________________________.

B. Look and write.

bookstore / buy a book

 Can ____

____?

 No, Ted. We _________________________________

____.

Aw. ____

____

A. Which planet is it? Read and write.

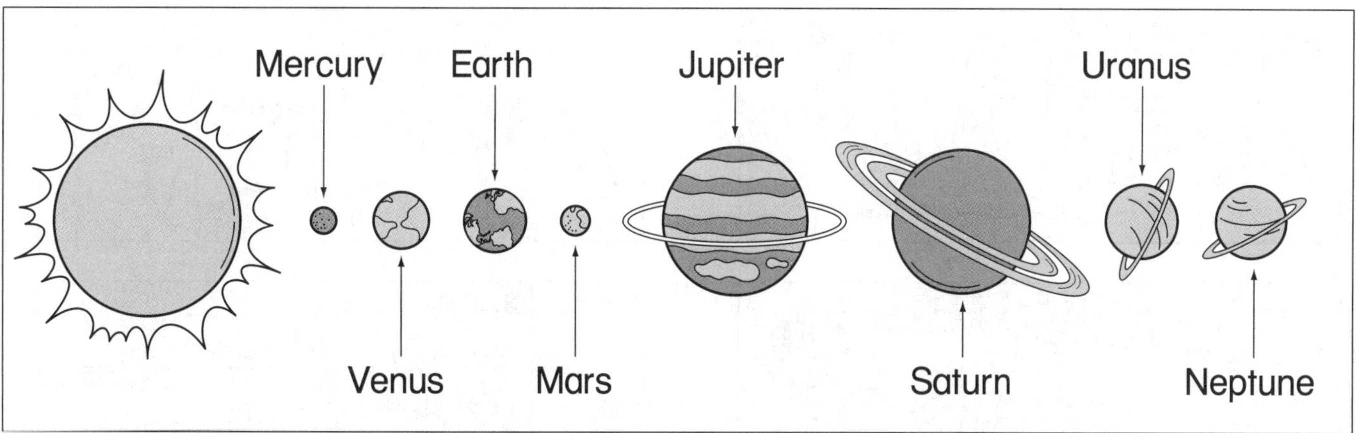

1. It's next to Mercury. It's smaller than Earth. **It's Venus.** _______________

2. It's next to Saturn, but it isn't Jupiter. **It's** _______________.

3. It's next to the smallest planet. It's smaller than Jupiter. _______________

4. It's the smallest planet. It's next to Venus. _______________

5. It's next to Jupiter. It's bigger than Uranus. _______________

6. It's next to Mars, but it isn't next to Venus. _______________

7. It's our planet. We live here. _______________

8. It's next to Jupiter, but it isn't next to Uranus. _______________

B. Write the names of the planets.

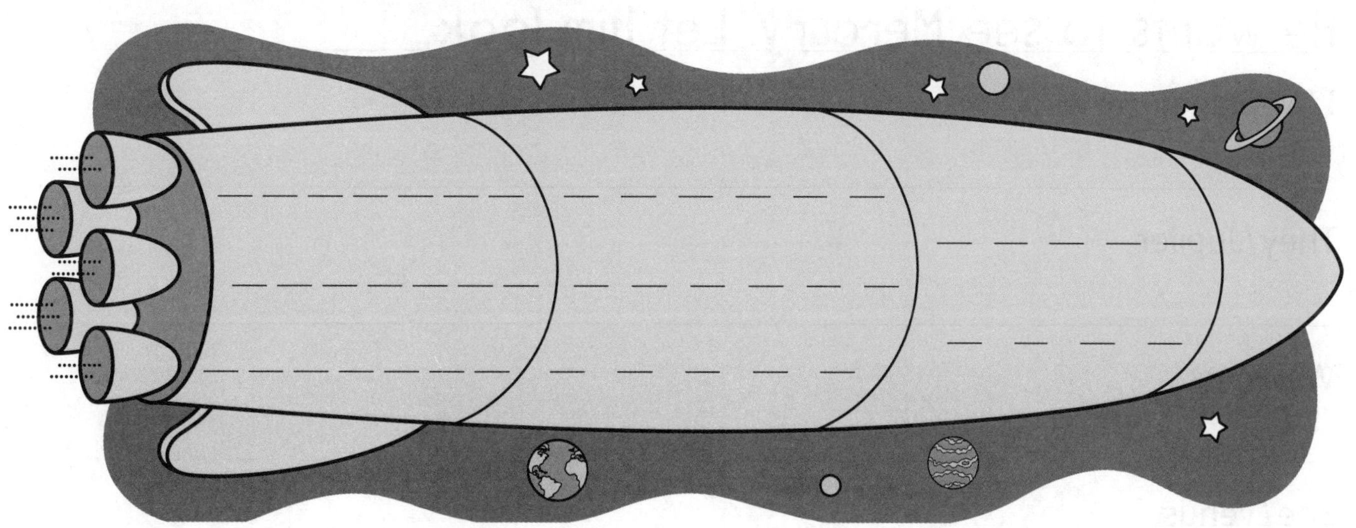

A. Number the sentences.

_____ She wants to see Mercury.
Let her look.

_____ He wants to see Saturn.
Let him look.

_____ I want to see Neptune.
Let me look.

_____ They want to see Venus.
Let them look.

B. Read and write.

1. she → <u>her</u>   2. I → _____   3. we → _____   4. they → _____   5. he → _____

C. Read and write.

1. He / Mercury

<u>He wants to see Mercury. Let him look.</u>

2. I / Neptune

____

3. They / Jupiter

____

4. We / Mars

____

5. She / Venus

____

A. Does it have **oi** or **oy**? Write and match.

1. R____ is a b____. J____ce is a girl. ●

2. R____ p____nted at the ____sters
   in the f____l.

3. R____ b____led some ____sters. ●

4. J____ce br____led some ____sters. ●

5. J____ce wanted s____ sauce and
   R____ wanted ____l.

6. They ate the ____sters and jumped
   for j____.

B. Follow the **oy** words.

12

A. **Fill in the blanks. Then number the sentences.**

together	dance	practice	have	dancing	do
dancer	idea	That's	enough	well	

1 You __________ really well.

Sure you __________.
You're a good __________. ___

___ But I don't practice __________.

Well, __________ makes perfect. ___

___ __________ a great idea. Thanks.

Thanks. I love __________. ___

___ I don't dance very __________.

I __________ an __________.
Let's practice __________. ___

B. **Look and write.**

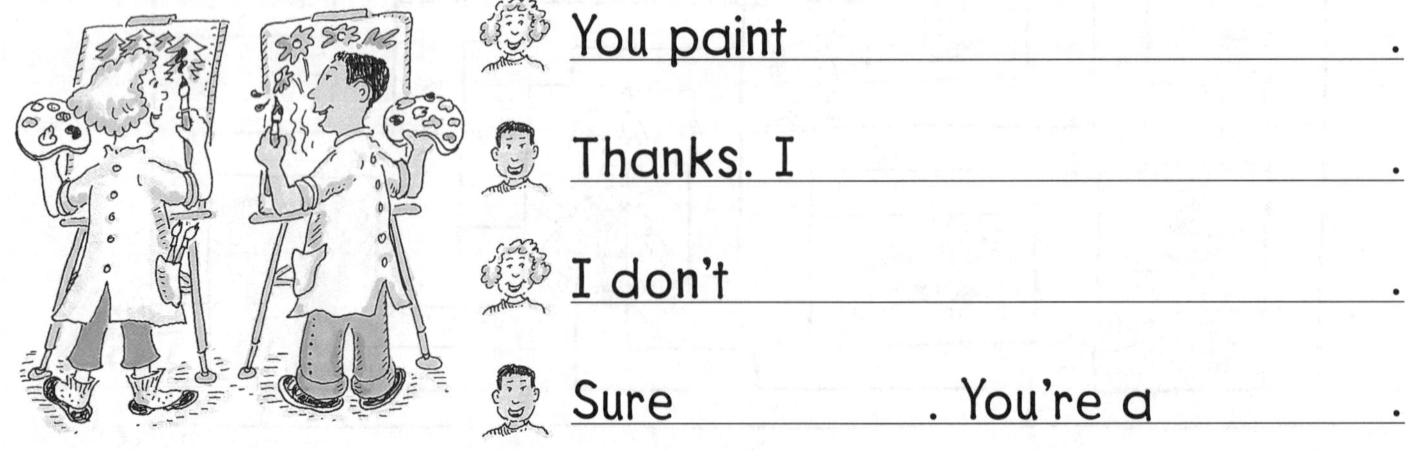

You paint _________________________________.

Thanks. I _________________________________.

I don't _________________________________.

Sure _____________. You're a _____________.

A. Read and match.

1. musician
2. nurse
3. computer programmer
4. engineer
5. artist

B. Read and write.

Today is Sunday. What are they going to do on Monday?

1.  She's a musician. __She's going to__ _________________________.

2.  He's a vet. _________________________

3.  They're engineers. _________________________

4.  She's a computer programmer. _________________________

5.  They're artists. _________________________

6. 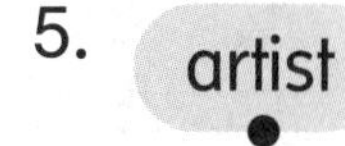 He's a nurse. _________________________

A. Read and write.

1. Why does she want to be ________________________________?
   Because she likes ________________________________.

2. Why does he want to be ________________________________?
   ____

3. Why do they want to be ________________________________?
   ____

4. Why does he want to be ________________________________?
   ____

5. Why does she want to be ________________________________?
   ____

6. Why does she want to be ________________________________?
   ____

B. Your turn. Read and write.

Why do you want to be a ________________________________?

Because ________________________________.

A. Read and write. Use some letters twice.

ar	au	er	or	ow	ou	oi	ur	ir	oo

1. 

P_____l and Patty went shopping.
P_____l bought a sh_____t. Patty
bought a p_____se. The cl_____k was
very happy!

2. 

Walt c_____ked lunch today. He
b_____led some spaghetti. "Yum!" said
Sue. But there was a c_____n in the
spaghetti and a mark_____ in the salad!

3. 

Carl went to the p_____k. He ate
d_____t with a f_____k and got very
d_____ty. He saw a d_____k cl_____d
and thought, "I can take a sh_____er in
the rain!"

B. Do they both have the same vowel sound? Look and write ✓ or ✗.

1.	2.	3.	4.
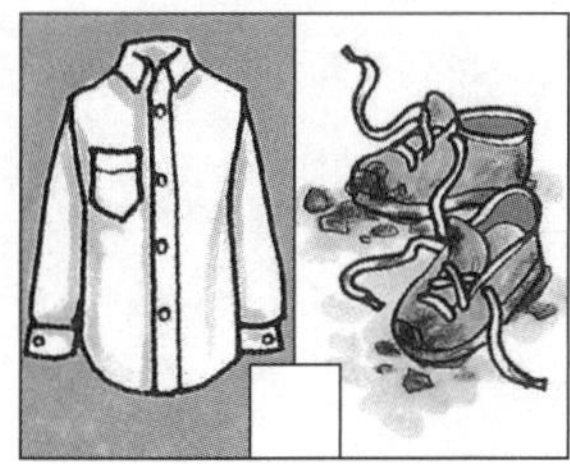			

A. Read and match. Then fill in the blanks.

> dancer   easy   dancing   great   idea   myself

1. Was it hard? •

    • Sure you do. You're a good
    _________________________.

2. I don't dance very well. •

    • That's a great ________________.
    Thanks.

3. Did you see all the planets and • stars?

    • Thanks. I love ________________.

4. I have an idea. Let's practice together. •

    • No, it was ________________.

5. Wow! What a cool kite! •

    • Yeah! That was a ________________ show.

6. You dance really well. •

    • Thanks. I made it ________________.

B. Circle the odd word.

1. | collect stickers | artist | paint | cycle |

2. | build things | Mars | Mercury | Jupiter |

3. | read comic books | build models | computer programmer | make movies |

4. | Venus | vet | Earth | Saturn |

5. | engineer | help animals | take care of people | take a nap |

6. | sing | cycle | paint | nurse |

A. Read. Then answer the questions.

Hi. My name is Burt. This is Matt and this is Nell. Matt is twelve years old. Nell is eleven. Matt likes building things. He wants to be an engineer. Matt likes playing the violin, but he doesn't like singing. Nell likes singing, but she doesn't like playing the violin. She wants to be an artist. She likes drawing.

1. Does Matt like singing?

   ____

2. Why does Nell want to be an artist?

   ____

3. Does Nell like playing the violin?

   ____

4. Why does Matt want to be an engineer?

   ____

B. Look and write.

1. 

   _____ster

2. 

   dess_____t

3. 

   b_____d

4. 

   p_____se

5. 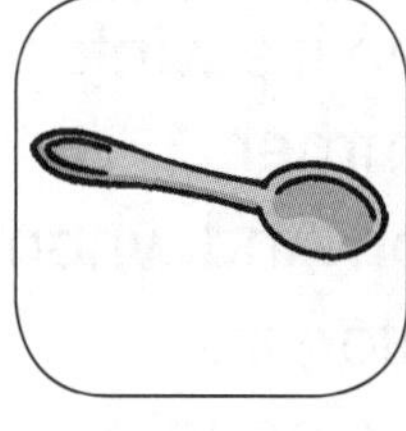

   sp_____n

6. 

   cl_____d

7. 

   p_____nt

8. 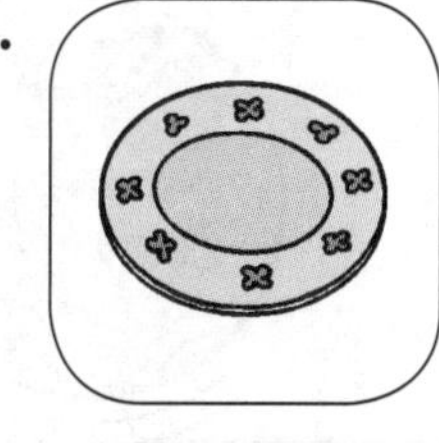

   s_____cer

A. Read and match.

1. 

2. 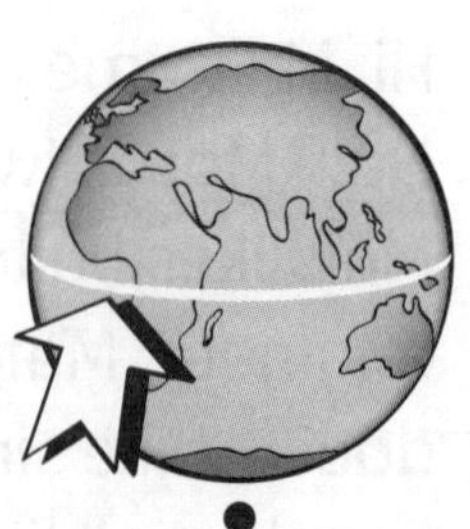

3. 

globe   north   east   equator   west   south   compass

4. 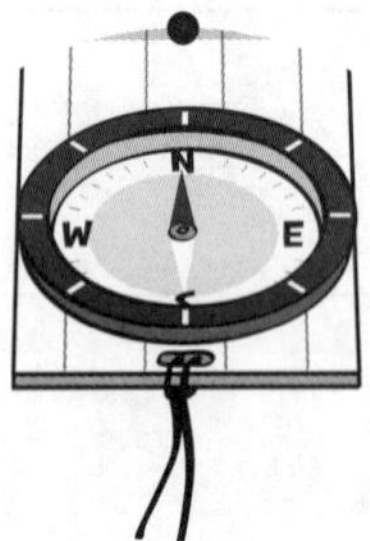

5. 

6. 

7. 

B. Read and write.

1. 

This is a map. Can you see N, S, E, and W on the _____________? The mountains are _____________ of the lake. The forest is _____________ of the lake.

2. 

This is a _____________. Look! Can you see the _____________? When it's winter north of the equator, it's summer _____________ of the equator. And when it's winter south of the equator, it's summer _____________ of the equator.

A. Read and match.

1. What are you eating?
2. Let me help you.
3. What time is it?
4. Where's the music room?
5. What kind of juice do you want?
6. I'm looking for the museum. Is it far?

- Pineapple juice, please.
- Not really.
- It's across from the library.
- Thanks. Be careful.
- Rice.
- Seven o'clock. It's time for breakfast.

B. Read and match.

1. Can we go to the snack bar?
2. Wow! What a cool kite!
3. Are you sure?
4. It's not cute. It's scary.
5. You dance really well.
6. We won! We won!

- I'm positive.
- Thanks. I love dancing.
- Don't worry. It won't hurt you.
- Congratulations!
- Thanks. I made it myself.
- No, we don't have time.

Word Time Review

Find 14 activities. Then write the words.

1. ride a horse
2. ___________________
3. ___________________
4. ___________________
5. ___________________
6. ___________________
7. ___________________
8. ___________________
9. ___________________
10. ___________________
11. ___________________
12. ___________________
13. ___________________
14. ___________________

A. Match and write.

1. What are you going to have? •   • Yes, ______________________.

2. She drank soda pop. •   • I'm ______________________ tacos.

3. What did she do? •   • ______ not going to see a movie.

4. He'll play in the leaves in the fall. •   • She ______________ win a prize.

5. Did they watch the sunrise? •   • ______ won't ______________ the beach.

6. I'm going to rent a DVD. •   • She swept ______________________.

B. Write and match.

1. Why ______________ to be an artist? •   • bigger than the dolphin.

2. ______________ he like to do? •   • Let her look.

3. Which one is the ______________? •   • but I don't like cycling.

4. She ______________ Mars. •   • Because I like drawing.

5. ______ like painting, •   • He likes to go sailing.

6. ______ whale ______ •   • The giraffe is the tallest.

A. What vowel sound does it have? Look and match.

1. 
2. 
3. 
4. 

aw •   ar •   ur •   er •   ou •   oo •   oi •   or •

5. 
6. 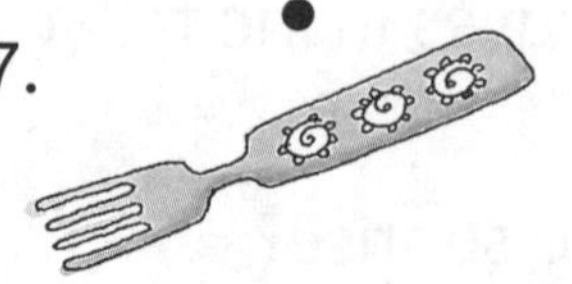
7. 
8.

B. Which word has a different -ed sound? Read and circle.

1.
walked
kissed
weeded
chopped

2.
planted
cleaned
invited
dusted

3.
called
played
baked
stayed

4.
waited
dusted
roasted
washed

C. Read.

Mark likes to look at the moon. His friends Paul and Roy like to look at it, too. On Monday, Mark invited Paul and Roy for dinner. They cooked some food and made apple pie for dessert. Then they cleaned up. Mark said, "Let's hurry! It's time to look at the moon!" They climbed the mountain by the town and looked at the moon and stars. It was a good night, and Mark was happy.

A

again	39
answer	30
antibiotic ointment	15
art class	24
artist	55
ate	7

B

baked	8
bandage	15
barn	32
because	59
beetle	21
bicycle	21
big	32
bigger	33
bird	49
blister	23
blocks	16
boil	53
bottle	19
bought	7
boy	53
bread	4
break	15
breakfast	1
broom	42
brown	38
build a model	47
build a snowman	25
build things	55
building	48
burn	15
burrito(s)	21
butter	23
buy a donut	17
buy tickets	6

C

called	8
careful	9
carnivore	45
cashier	31
cast	15
catch the bus	50
chair	4
cheetah	36
chimpanzee	36
chopped	8
clean the tent	2
cleaned	3
clerk	49
climb a mountain	2
climbed	3
collect stickers	47
collecting	48
compass	60
computer programmer	55
congratulations	41
consumer	45
cook	42
cook breakfast	2
cooked	3
corn	34
crab	32
crawl	27
cry	4
curry	21
cut	15
cute	31
cycle	50
cycling	51

D

dance	54
dance teacher	54
dancer	54
delicious	20
dessert	49
did	3
didn't	3
dinner	24
division	30
divided by	30
do the laundry	10
dolphin	32
drank	7
draw	55
drawing	56
drink soda pop	6
drum	4
dusted	12

E

Earth	51
east	60
easy	46
eat cotton candy	6
eel	32
elephant	36
engineer	55
enough	5
equation	30
equator	60

F

fall (n.)	25
fall (v.)	27
far	16
farm	34
fast	32
faster	33
fat	36
fattest	37
fed	11
feed the pets	10
fish	4
flower	4
food chain	45
fork	34
french fry	21
french fries	21

G

get a haircut	17
gift shop	50
giraffe	36
globe	60
go fishing	40
go horseback riding	40
go on a ride	6
go sailing	40
go skiing	25
go to the beach	25
going to	18
gown	38
green	4
greeted	12
guess what	35

H

had	7
hang up the clothes	10
hard	46
have lunch	6
heavy	9
he'll	26
help animals	55
helping	56

her	52
herbivore	45
him	52
hot dog(s)	21
house	38
hung	11

I

I'll	26
ice pack	15
iced tea	21
in-line skate	40
invited	12
it was close	39

J

joy	56
Jupiter	54
just a little	20

K

kind of	5
kissed	8

L

laugh at jokes	2
laughed	3
laundry	26
left	16
lemonade	21
library	24
listen to music	40
listen to stories	2
listened	3
little	20
lobster	23
look	42
love	57

M

made 11
mail a letter 17
make a movie 50
make the bed 10
make up your mind 31
making 51
marker 60
Mars 54
math 24
Mercury 54
missed 39
monkey 35
moon 42
mother 4
mouse 38
mouth 38
multiplication 30
multiply by 30
music room 24
musician 55
myself 46
my treat 5

N

need 49
Neptune 54
nice game 39
north 60
not really 16
nurse 55

O

octopus 32
oil 53
omnivore 45
oyster 53

P

paint 47
painting 48
photographer 54
pick apples 25
plane 4
planets 53
plant flowers 25
planted 12
play badminton 40
play cards 2
play in the leaves 25
play Ping-Pong 47
play the violin 55
played 3
playing 56
point 53
poodle 19
positive 31
practice makes perfect 54
present 4
producer 45
program computers 55
programming 56
pudding 20
puddle 19
purse 49
put away the groceries 10

R

read a comic book 47
reading 48
rent a DVD 17
ride the bus 17
right 16

S

Saturn 51
saucer 27
saw 7
scary 35
see a movie 17
see a show 6
set the table 10
shark 32
she'll 26
shirt 49
short 36
shortest 37
show 46
shower 57
shut 35
sing 47
singing 48
skateboard 9
slide 4
slow 32
slower 33
small 32
smaller 33
smile 4
snack bar 50
snake 36
sneeze 4
snorkel 40
south 60
spaghetti 21
spoon 4
spring 25
stars 50
storm 34
straight 24
strain 15
string 46
strong 9
subject 24
summer 25

sweep the floor 10
swept 11

T

taco(s) 21
take a taxi 17
take care of people 55
take out the garbage 10
take photographs 54
take pictures 6
taking 48
talk 27
tall 36
tallest 37
than 33
them 52
they'll 26
thin 36
thinnest 37
three 4
tiger 23
time for 1
time to go 31
told you so 20
took 7
town 38
tree 4
try some 20
turn 16
turtle 36

U

uncle 19
Uranus 51
us 52

V

Venus 51
vet 55
visit a friend 17

W

waited 12
wake up 1
wash the pots and pans 2
washed 3
watch out 9
watch the sunrise 2
watched 3
we'll 26
weeded 12
went 7
west 60
whale 32
why 56
win a prize 6
winter 25
won 7
won't 26
wood 42
word problem 30

Y

yard 34
you'll 26
you're kidding 46